THE BEEKEEPER

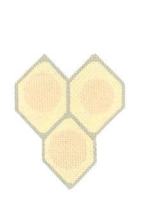

THE BEEKEEPER

Mr Davies is a beekeeper.
His first job every morning
is to check the hives.
The hives are different colours.
Bees can recognize colours.
They can tell their own hive by its colour.

THE BEEKEEPER

Inside the hives, there are frames.
The hard-working bees
fill the frames with honey.
Mr Davies wears special beekeepers' clothes
to protect himself from the bees.
He uses a bee smoker
to gently blow puffs of smoke into the hive.
The smoke quiets the bees,
and he is able to remove the honey frames
without the bees attacking him.
Sometimes a bee will sting him on the hand,
but he is used to that and it doesn't bother him.

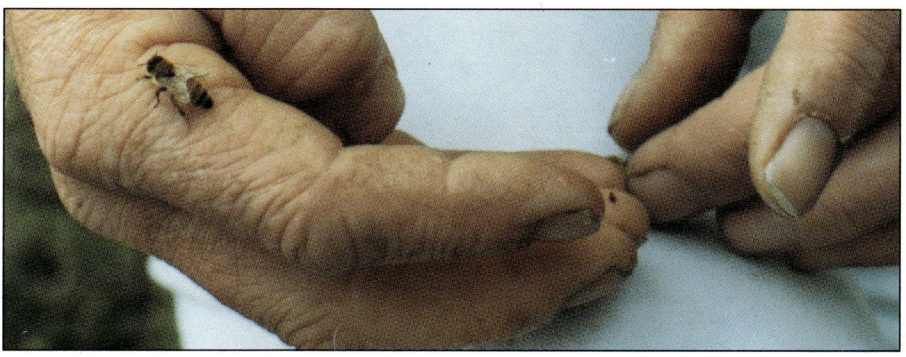

THE BEEKEEPER

The bees are not happy when he takes
their stored honey
from the hive.
They form into clusters
to try to work out what to do next.
They will settle down when he puts
empty frames back into their hive
and will soon be very busy
filling the new frames with honey.

THE BEEKEEPER

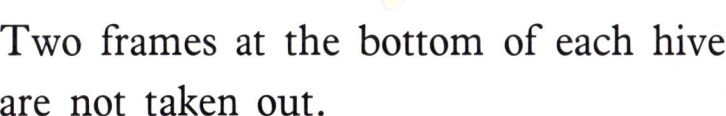

Two frames at the bottom of each hive
are not taken out.
These are the special brood frames,
where the bees rear their young.
If you look carefully,
you can see eggs and grubs in the little cells.
The cells without caps on them
are filled with yellow pollen.
The brood nest is always in the middle
of the brood frame.
Here the worker bees feed and nurse the young.

This large bee is a drone.
The worker bees kill off
the drones when winter
is near because they want
to save the stored honey
to feed the young
and themselves.

10

THE BEEKEEPER

The frames filled with honeycomb
are carefully lifted from the hives.
A heated electric capping knife
is used to take the wax cappings
off the outside of the frames.
Some of this wax will go to be made
into cosmetics, floor polish, or candles.

THE BEEKEEPER

The frames are then placed into an extractor. The extractor takes the honey off the frames by spinning the frames around and around very, very quickly.

The honey is strained from the extractor, heated slightly, and pumped into big drums. Any bits of pollen or leftover specks of wax come to the surface of the warm honey and are skimmed off with a special float.

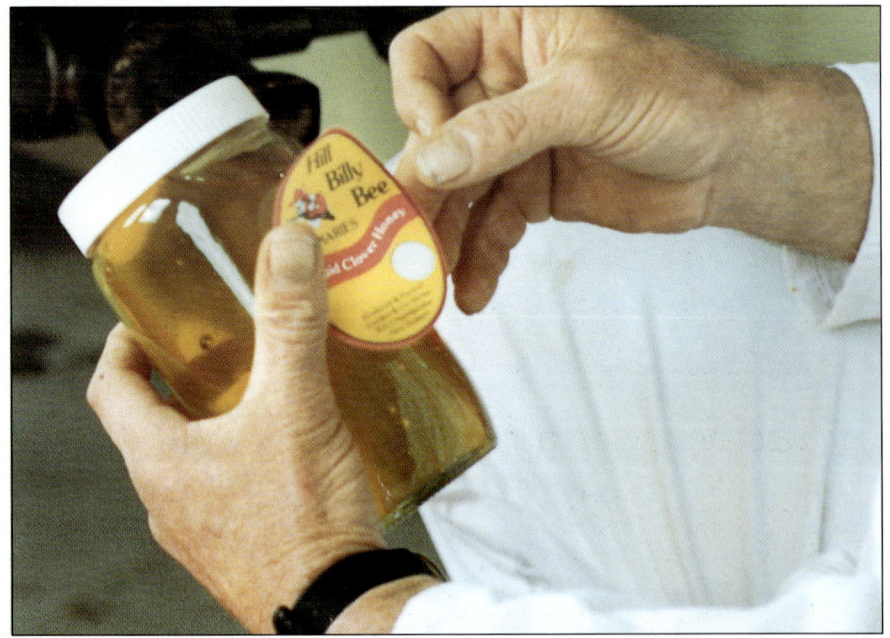

THE BEEKEEPER

The honey is poured into jars.
The lids are put on,
and Mr Davies' "Hill Billy Bee" labels
are stuck on to the outside.
The honey is now ready to be sold,
and Mr Davies is ready for his lunch.
What does he have for lunch?
Yes! Bread and honey!

THE BEEKEEPER GLOSSARY

BEE: An insect found just about everywhere in the world, apart from the two Poles. Of the 10,000 species, only the honeybee makes edible honey.

BROOD FRAME: Frame at the bottom of the hive, where the bees rear their young.

CELLS: Hexagonal-shaped compartments built by bees to hold nectar, pollen, eggs, and developing bees. There are about 25 cells in 2.5 square cm (1 square in) of honeycomb.

DRONE: A male honeybee.

EXTRACTOR: Machine used to separate honey from the comb.

FRAME: Removable shelves of a hive on which the workers build their honeycombs and brood cells.

GRUB: The larva stage of the bee's development. Twenty-one days after the egg is laid, an adult bee emerges from its cell.

HIVE: A structure with room for the bees' nest and space to store honey.

HONEY: A main product of the hive. Nectar collected from flowers by the worker bees is stored in their stomachs and later placed in the cells as honey.

HONEYCOMB: Cluster of six-sided compartments called cells.

POLLEN: Dust-like substance taken from flowers by the bees, stored in cells around the brood nest.

QUEEN BEE: Large female honeybee, capable of laying a thousand eggs a day. There is only one queen bee in the hive, and she is the mother of all the bees living in that hive.

SMOKER: Smoke-producing equipment used to quiet bees so the beekeeper can clear the hive.

WAX: Capping produced by bees to protect the cells. Beeswax is removed from honeycomb to make into candles, cosmetics, and polishes.

WORKER BEES: Usually several thousand in each hive who do all of the work of the hive. They build and clean the cells, gather nectar, and care for the young.